I

ON BROKEN NIGHTS LIKE THESE

Poetry

Heidi Thompson

Cover design by: Heidi Thompson
Edited by: Russell L. Ridgeway

CONTENTS

Title Page

Copyright

SHADOW CHILD   1

UNDERSTANDING YOU   3

YOU, MY UNIVERSE   4

RAINFALL   5

MIDNIGHT   6

WEARY BONES   7

REST EASY   8

NIGHTS LIKE THESE   9

WISE OLD EYES   11

THE THINGS I ASK   13

COMFORT IN YOU   15

JUDGEMENT DAY   17

FINDING HOME   19

MOON'S CHILD   20

BREATHE   22

APOCALYPSE   24

WATER'S EDGE   26

YELLOW   27

FORBIDDEN   29

PORTRAIT   30

THURSDAY   31

PETRICHOR   33

OBLIVION   35

LONESOME TRAVELLER   37

EPHEMERAL   39

HIRAETH   41

STAY   43

QUIET LOVE   44

HEAR ME   45

SUDDENLY   46

THE ORCHARD OF SILENT DEVOTION   48

REMINDERS   50

FIREFLIES   51

HAIKUS   53

This book is dedicated to my family.

SHADOW CHILD

On a cold and biting winter's eve,
A silent darkness falls.
A sheet of night to cover up
A small boy's helpless calls.

A little street, a winding road,
A car screeched to a halt.
Two polished shoes, small footsteps sound,
Up and down the asphalt.

A small window stood modest and hidden
At the far end of the cottage.
Though always drawn, the curtains seep the morning orange
glow,
Always, now, and every day,
A small boy sits alone.

The neighbour's house is deathly silent,
Loud snores drift up the stairs.
The light's been out for hours now,
The darkness reconciled.
But gazing out the steamed glass pane,
Dwells a Shadow Child.

He had no name, no friends, no home,
Just a house in which to roam,
A mind that reached up to the stars,
A heart no good alone.

Shadow Child had no friends,

"But that's okay", he said.
He sat alone in this darkened room,
As the night-time only spread.

No one knew of Shadow Child,
No one ever would.
That's what comes with haunting the shadows,
That, he understood.

How many words were left unsaid,
How many lay ahead?
How many men had bled to death,
How many had just fled?

When would someone come to save him?
Listen for his calls?
How many centuries left to wait
Amongst these cold brick walls?

Shadow Child was all but lost,
Shadow Child was scared.
But even if someone did find him,
Shadow Child was dead.

Budapest, December 5, 2022

UNDERSTANDING YOU

What is love,
If not a rose in a field of poppies?
If not a candle in the wavering dusk?
If not the end of all our stories?

What is love,
If not a beauty, if not a joy?
If not a gut-wrenching tragedy?
A proof of our mortality?

Why do I love?
Is it to hurt me? console me? tear me apart?
Should I leave or continue,
Until I wake with a start?

When will I love?
When will I see the miracle too?
When will I smile and know it is true?
For this isn't love, I feel it, I know.
You aren't who I'm supposed to forever follow.

Budapest, January 6, 2023

YOU, MY UNIVERSE

How can the Sun shine so bright as the light leaves your eyes?
How dare the ground be so warm as your hands turn so cold?
The Universe has no right to breathe so freely as you take your final breath.
Life goes on as you fall asleep and are lain down to rest,
But the universe I kept you in implodes within my chest.

Budapest, February 26, 2023

RAINFALL

The drops of rain
Like heartbroken angels
Falling from grace.
Like tears of prophecy
Baring the news
Of no tomorrow.
The grief of Heaven
Staining the earth
And bruising the flowers,
Projecting it's unsaid pain
On all that is still alive.
A lonely traveller
On a road from nowhere,
Leading him to the absent void.
He picked up his pace,
Wishing to stay dry,
But hungry, like a wayward child
Starving in this abandoned corner,
Aching for release.

Budapest, April 13, 2023

MIDNIGHT

A million bright, weary eyes
Blinking down at the earth,
Begging to be seen
But going forever unnoticed.
A thousand hungry sailors, lost and alone,
Sailing on the open sea,
An infinite, impenetrable void.
A hundred things I never got to say,
Before the thought slipped from my fragile grasp.
Ten ways it could have ended differently.
And one tear, just one,
That fell upon the earth
To water the anguish of the night.

Budapest, April 14, 2023

WEARY BONES

There was silence.
The kind that comforts,
Wrapping you within its arms
And protecting you in sleep.
The kind that lingers
In graveyards
Where the air hums the low,
Quiet hymn of weary bones,
The solemn note of sleep.
The sound of the wind
Rustling the leaves of an ageing oak.
Not a storm, just a gentle breeze
Brushing over the lonely headstones.
Like a mother comforting a frightened child,
Whispering a low reassurance
That everything will be okay.
The words seep into the hardened ground,
Sweet and earnest,
Soothing the fallen with its gentle melody.
A time to rest their weary bones,
Laden with years of unease
Dispersing in the heavens above.

Budapest, April 18, 2023

REST EASY

Your gaze locked upon my own,
Two deep, infinitely vast oceans.
And as I stared into them,
I knew that I was drowning.
A warm ray of sun gleamed
Somewhere just beneath the surface.
But the more I tried to reach it,
The further it slipped from my feeble grasp.
My words do not lie,
And I will sing you a lullaby
Every night for the rest of my life
If it'll mean you can sleep in peace.
And I swear I won't sleep
Ever again,
If it means I can stand guard by your side
While you dream of a love
You wouldn't have to hide.
And it means I can rest easy,
Knowing that you love me back.
Lay your weary head on my shoulder,
And rest your sunken eyes
That have seen far too much
Beyond the frayed shield of my love.
And as your hands turn to ice
And slip from my own trembling grasp,
Promise you'll sleep easy, knowing that
No matter how hidden in the evening hue,
My heart is lain there right beside you.
   -Budapest, April 24, 2023

NIGHTS LIKE THESE

Sometimes on dark, dreary nights like these
I sit at my desk by the faint glow of dawn,
And realize, in a faint flash of clarity,
Just how lonely it feels.
And on nights like these my thoughts drift,
Perhaps by accident, to you.
Sometimes, on lifeless days like these,
As I walk through the park, alone,
My gaze catches on a couple
Laughing airily as they go past,
Breathing in the sweet air of the early spring.
And, perhaps unwillingly, I imagine you beside me,
As we do the same.
Just recently, I've been thinking about you more.
It must be something
That reminds me of you
Every time I see someone smile,
Their face lighting up with childish joy.
Though perhaps you aren't so young anymore.
Sometimes, lying in bed with nothing to do but think,
I realize how little I've known you for.
Yet still,
When I think back to my sweetest moments of life,
In almost every one of them,
You are there beside me.
And sometimes, in quiet moments like these,
When the air is threatening to choke me
With the weight of my uncertainties,

Hesitantly, with eyes closed against the urgency of life,
I imagine the sun setting, somewhere far from here.
All sweet pinks and purples and vibrant oranges,
The waves simmering past more weightlessly than my heart,
Buried beneath the suffocating layers of your absence.
And, seeing your tender smile,
All too real in my presence,
Cautiously, and only when drunk full on your joy,
I dare hope that my feelings aren't in vain.
And, in moments and only moments like these,
I consider writing you a letter,
Every word entwined with timid and quiet yearning,
And a hope for reciprocation.
But alas, the moment passes,
And I sober up once again.
Because as soon as my gaze drifts
From your delicately simple eyes
My heart caves in and gives way
For fear to drag my soul to the depths
Again and again
For the rest of my days.

Stjørdal, April 31, 2023

WISE OLD EYES

The memory of that first day
is still far too vivid before my eyes.
It was mere seconds before my life began,
in a flash of hesitant smiles
and a face so young but so wise,
though of course I hadn't known that yet.
Holding you in my arms for the first time
felt like finally breathing in
after so many eternities spent choking on the air around me.
And seeing you smile, every single time,
looked like a butterfly spreading its wings of gold,
flying off after years of captivity,
held hostage by its fear of heights.
And so, time passed.
It seemed so slow at the time,
moments halting on every shared glance
in the moonlit summer nights.
But August arrived swiftly,
with its icy winds and greying clouds
chilling me to my bones.
And I found myself,
mind frozen by the frost
settling on my heart,
sitting by old sheets, gaze still set on your own,
and remembering with quiet sorrow
the first time you did the same.
Those wise old eyes reflecting universes
and worlds no man could ever see

with eyes so pure as my own.
At the time I laughed at
how odd they seemed
on such young shoulders.
But today, I see the finished picture,
with all its cracks and imperfections.
A woeful smile shics its way onto my face
when I realize: you have always been like this.
I sat silent as you mustered up
your final strands of youth
in a gaze not so young
and playful as it once was,
but still filled
to the last drop with your essence.
You had made me the last picture
put before your unseeing eyes,
closing, like every night before, to sleep.
...
This morning I awoke, but I felt cold.
It feels strange to search for your presence
in a room without you there.
Your side of the bed was missing you,
but still wrinkled from a time when it hadn't been.
And tonight, I went to sleep alone,
my heart heaving with the unfamiliar weight
of your absence.
But, despite the distance feeling so very far,
I know I went to sleep sleeping under your star.

Stjørdal, May 1, 2023

THE THINGS I ASK

I've got a list of all the things
I still have to do,
before I close my eyes upon this world
and can finally rest in peace.
First, I'll have to thank you
over and over until my eyes brim with tears,
and then once more,
yet it still won't be enough.
Then I want to show you
just how much I care,
with a handmade gift sealed by a note
where I can once again write:
thank you.
And I'll remind you every day
of just how much this means,
because I never make gifts,
and I never write letters,
and I could never understand how I feel,
unless it's what I feel for you.
Then I'll muster up all the courage
I never knew I had,
and I'll tell you straight up,
(Like you hadn't already known),
exactly what it is
that caused me to lose my tongue,
and forget myself in your presence.
Next, I'll make you listen to
every single song I've ever heard

that makes me think of you.
And I'll make you stay up 'till 3 am,
like the thought of you did to me
for so many years before.
The next day I'll invite you
to walk along the pier, hand in hand,
eating ice creams and gazing at the seagulls flying past,
gliding weightlessly towards the Sun
like our young and infatuated hearts.
Then at night, when the birds have left,
and silence sits above us,
I can fall asleep beside you,
reassured that I'll never be alone,
ever again.
The last thing on my to-do list,
the last thing I'll ever ask,
is to stay with you long enough
to watch your hair grow grey,
and every passing year
add new wrinkles to your sunlit face,
but for your gaze to still hold
the same child-like adoration
when held upon my own
as it did so many years ago,
when we were only teenage hearts
filled with passions and ambitions
that came true in each other's eternal presence.

Stjørdal, May 2, 2023

COMFORT IN YOU

I know that I'm a bad liar.
I could never lie to your face,
And say you aren't all I think about
On sleepless summer nights.
I wish I could tell you that everything I do
Isn't simply to see you smile,
Even if just for a single moment.
I can't decide if the comfort of your presence
Is love,
Or just a young heart's need for exploration,
But you've only been gone for a single day,
And my bones are already yearning
To see your face alight with joy
And hear your hopeful voice again.
I wish I knew how to show you
Just how much you mean to me
When you give me refuge in your heart.
And recently, I've learnt what it feels like
To want to live
Every time you tell a stupid joke
That makes both of us giggle for hours,
Until I lose my breath,
And my cheeks ache from my ecstasy,
And my soul feels completely weightless
From effortlessly loving every piece of you
That I can touch.
Whenever you get sad
And forget what it feels like

To touch the ground, and swim
In the motherly warmth it emits,
I can be your anchor
That pulls you back to Earth.
But sometimes, I wonder what it'd be like
To lose our grasps
And sail off together,
To explore uncharted seas
And oceans our childish hearts
Have never known before.
My soul aches to hold your heart in my hands,
But every time I inch a little closer,
I'm scared you'll drift out of reach,
And the stars I sleep under every night
Will turn to dust before my stinging eyes.
Sometimes, when my shoulders adorn
These torturous thoughts like capes,
Though deep down I know it's not your fault,
I just wish you'd stop doing this to me.
I wish this was a love story,
But for now, I suppose I'll just pretend.
I guess that's just what love feels like
When you are young and in love with a friend.

Oslo, May 7, 2023

JUDGEMENT DAY

When the world begins to end
And all the walls come
Crashing down around us,
I'll stand on the frontlines
When the Judgement comes
If that's what it takes to keep you safe.
You know I'm no Angel,
Not anymore,
But since there's no tomorrow
I will be your hero
If you ever change your mind about us.
So maybe I'll fall
From the grace of Heaven,
Though I can't bring myself to care.
'Cause at least I'll know I fell
To lift you up.
For you I'll drench my heart in gasoline
And watch with a smile as it burns
To a smouldering pile of burning ashes,
But it'll still remind me
Of you.
'Cause baby, you know our love is like fire,
Destructive but alive.
And with the light of a thousand flaming suns,
We'll watch as it burns this world to the ground.
Because this world will never love you
Like I do.
There will be no tomorrow,

And we have nothing left to lose,
But our love.
Hold me closer, for tonight's the final night.
To die within your arms would be
the only way that's right.

Oslo, May 7, 2023

FINDING HOME

My love, why do you cry?
Does the Sun not shine on your face like it used to?
Do the blades of grass not caress your skin
And the wind not hum you a low, sweet lullaby
To remind you you're alive?
Have you forgotten a time when you lay right here,
On the shore of this pretty creek,
Listening as the sweet waters whispered stories
Of long, strange adventures,
Having found comfort in existence
So far from their home?
The clouds brim with tears
Every time you say you don't deserve their love.
Bathing in the woeful beauty of your soul,
So frayed and fragile, but oh so alive,
They wonder why you can't see it too.
The soil beneath you grounds you to Earth
When your mind is floating away,
And the Angels lend you their wings
So you can learn to fly
When your heart is sinking in the ground.
Give me your heart and I'll show you
Every detail that causes a smile to
Bloom on my face.
And I promise, as long as you're here,
It will shine.

Budapest, May 13, 2023

MOON'S CHILD

The day now sleeps,
And the yawning moon rises once again.
Tired and weary mountain tops
Reach high above the broken songs,
And boiling tears of the people below.
I beckon thee, my child.
Look beyond your troubled head and see
The fading summer skies.
Your mother, the weeping moon
Washes your troubled souls clean
With hushed lunar melodies,
And odes to your fragile and broken minds.
Her lullaby entwines with sincere, quiet words:
Lay your aching head
On the sweet meadows of her lap
And rest within her loving arms,
Basking in the warmth of her moonlit touch.
Your eyes are caved in,
Lonely taverns of longing
For a life of peace that you could never find.
My love, I know your days weigh on your heart
Like a sinking ship on the infinite oceans
Of your mind.
Your rapid thoughts are the angry waves
That will one day knock you down.
Floating is getting harder, my dear,
So just breathe, breathe, breathe.
The Sun won't offer you comfort

When you are locked in here once again,
Tears staining your youthful face.
On broken nights like these
I beckon thee, sweet child,
For the moon glows a bit brighter
Every time that you are near.
The seeds, too, slumber beneath the soil,
And the feather of an angel floats
weightlessly toward you,
Pleading you to listen to its words;
It's time to start dreaming.
Come home to us, sweet child of mine,
The Mother Moon awaits you with open arms,
And a gaze so tender and bright.
Until then, though, just sleep on, my love.
I promise, I'll watch over you tonight.

Budapest, May 22, 2023

BREATHE

You think I don't see the way
Your eyes darken on lonely nights?
You think I don't notice
Them brim with tears
When I tell you I love you
And you tell me to stop
Doing this to myself?
Perhaps in another universe
In a language different than our own
I'd have the strength to say it back,
And prove you wrong once more.
You think I wasn't there to witness
Every time you crumbled to the ground
In tiny, fractured pieces
Of a man who once was?
You were wrong, my love,
For I was always there to pick them up.
I gaze into your eyes and I see
The war raging deep inside
The taverns of your heart.
I see it, because it's my thought that
Leads your troops into battle.
Close your stinging eyes and tell me,
Just for a moment,
Every worry that weighs on your mind
And turns your innocent dreams
Into raging monsters of the night.
You think I don't see the hope,

Tender and fragile,
held protectively close to your heart.
Just this once I ask you
To look through the haze, and just
Breathe, breathe, breathe.
I know the summer air fills you with yearning
To heal the bleeding wounds
That your troubles have carved into your back.
Well, it's a start, my love,
And I want you to see,
I'm determined to make it work.

Budapest, May 23, 2023

APOCALYPSE

I've waited on you for so many years,
In so many ways,
For so many days.
Since then, my gaze has darkened,
And my smile faltered,
But it ignited once more
When you returned to me.
I remember the first time we stood here,
By the edge of this shy creek,
And I will always remember today,
Blue, sun kissed skies turning grey,
And the grass melting away
Under our calloused touch.
The world doesn't smile down at us,
Singing songs of our eternity in her presence.
The dusk that settled on heavy hearts
Is the only proof we need:
The world is ending, my dear.
We're still so young.
Just yesterday, we were wishing upon constellations,
Sharing dreams under moonlit skies,
And laughing 'till we both were breathless,
And our hearts beat effortlessly in our chests.
Even now, I can't help the smile
Creeping cautiously onto my face,
Hiding behind the faint shadows of smoke.
Our worlds have ended so many times,
Yet we built them up from the ashes.

Now there's truly no way to stop it,
So why does this not feel like a goodbye?

Transylvania, June 3, 2023

WATER'S EDGE

Gentle, foaming waves reach up,
And break against the hardened bay.
All soft pinks and blues,
A perfect mirror of the sky.
Looking up, in every breaking cloud
I see you gazing back at me,
Sending every remaining ray of sun
To warm me like the hearth.
I will never grow tired of
Sitting here beside you.
Bare, pale feet digging into the sun-warmed sand,
Drinking in every last morsel,
The quiet honesty in your sight.
In the mirror of your eyes
I see the man I want to be.
All soft smiles and quiet temper,
Laughing patiently at my every blunder,
Tripping over my words,
Like an animal born anew
With every gaze sent my way
From the golden pools of your eyes.
You are made of stardust,
Always floating weightlessly
Towards the ink-black kingdom above.
And I'll forever be the drunken moth,
Fluttering blindly toward your light.

Transylvania, June 9, 2023

YELLOW

Look at the stars
In the darkest corners of the night.
They watch over you when you're asleep in bed,
A shining halo above your head,
Look at how they shine for you,
Gleaming yellow in an endless void of blue.
Look at the sun as it lights up
Every crevice of your heart,
But leaves you cold and restless in the night,
For that is when I find my way in.
The sunflowers turned toward the blazing sun,
And listened close in that familiar, naive awe,
At the tales that she sung.
I'd listen to everything you say,
So that even just for a single day
You could be my blinding sun.
You could set my heart aflame at let it
Tread across my chest,
Licking at my skin and
Turning my bones to ash.
Sit beside me, watch the fire burn,
Shrivel up and turn to coal
Any wisdom that we earn.
Yellow embers lick away my soul.
Just leave my bones to melt away,
I didn't need them anyway.
You stare at me with those hardened cat-eyes,
Their yellow embers

Piercing through the sulking hush of the night.
You're searching every crevice of my mind,
And I'm sorry, but you won't find me back here.
Can you still see in the dark?
The crust leaves drifted from the tree
On old, unsteady wings,
Weighed to the ground by a year of their sorrow.
You didn't even hear them drop to the ground,
And they were all yellow.

Shoreham by Sea, July 3, 2023

FORBIDDEN

How far are you willing to fall for us?
How much are you willing to give for love?
Come closer, I promise you'll be safe in these arms,
You know Heaven can't keep us apart.
Let's set fire to the lonely night,
And watch as our entire lives are turned to dust.
God knows I've given enough,
And yet still, I am looking up.

Shoreham by Sea, July 5, 2023

PORTRAIT

He smiles at the old lady next door,
As he passes her on his way down the street.
He laughs at the jokes his father tells occasionally.
Knows, if he does not, he'll count the weight of his silence
In the purpling bruises of his poisonous touch.

He tells a false and weighted joke of his own
When queried upon these by the pained face of his lover.
Only in solidarity does he dare break the dams
Brought on by his own boiling blood.
Every night he lets it spill, hoping it will cleanse him
Of his primal curse.

He smiles softly at his weeping brother,
When meanwhile the coiling snake of dusk wraps itself around
his throat.
He whispers honey-sweet promises he knows he couldn't keep,
To let him know they'll both make it our unscathed.
His brother brightens, too young yet to see the empty in those
eyes.

He holds him close.
Gazes with a bittersweet reminiscence at the portrait of his past,
The haunting joy the boy's face still beholds.
He hopes with every battered shard of hope he still has left
That his brother will never understand.

Shoreham by Sea, July 12, 2023

THURSDAY

I really don't like Thursdays.
To my reddened eyes it seems only yesterday
That you were dragged away to death by the weight of your sorrow,
And I watched, gaping, as you disappeared.

You died on a Thursday.
On these days especially, I can't be consoled.
The misty, dull skies weep in beat to my stuttering heart.
The moment the ghostly wisp of your tender touch brushes over me,
It, too, shall be allowed to pause one last time.

Quiet lines, bowed head, I sit here on my own,
On the bench that once was ours.
When did the place that once held the feathers of two singing birds
Become burdened with tears and this single, lonely song?

A tired willow weeps somewhere above your bed.
It stands on weary and unsteady feet,
And its head bows closer to you at every breath of the wind,
To kiss you in farewell.

I sit here, too, and yearn to see you reach up,
And pull me closer for one last touch
Under the restless and fading skies.

HEIDI THOMPSON

One of these cold Thursdays I know in my heart,
Oblivion shall come to take me too,
Back between your warm two arms.

You know all too well; I have no other desire.
So, when the stars, the stars come beckoning,
We reunite -- arms around each other one last time,
We set off together into the sun.

Shoreham by Sea, July 12, 2023

PETRICHOR

The sun fades, and the dusk creeps its way
Into my trembling heart.
The rain has started up again.
It's been a while, but the tears come with practiced ease,
As if it were only yesterday that I discovered
You were leaving.

A single drop at first.
White-clad doctors with impassive faces told us the news
In hushed, sorrow-sewn tones.
You embraced me in attempt of comfort,
But all I could think about
Was when you would be letting go.

A few more tears came after that,
To water your fevered skin and chapped-lipped smile,
As every passing day sickness drew the clean-cut waves
Of the old ocean onto your forehead.

It all went too fast after that,
Leaving me reeling and snatching for a stolen breath.
Your ephemeral life slipped from between my fingers like a fine
silk.
And not long afterwards
The sky above us broke its dam,
Allowing your soul to drift up with the tide,

To the eternally sunny summer skies above.

The earth was dry a long time after that.
It made me wonder how you fared, if you still were.
But today, for one final time, you sang to the stars,
From closer than you ever have before.
The petrichor filled my lungs as I sat.
For the first time in the years since you've been gone,
I allow myself to wonder:
Are the skies treating you right?

Shoreham by Sea, July 13, 2023

OBLIVION

I've been standing here a while.
Tear tracks have begun to carve their way into your cheeks,
But I don't know what has caused them,
And you still refuse to tell me why.

The salty waves wash away at my bare feet.
It's cold. I don't quite seem to notice, though.
You seem sad, and I yearn to wrap my arms around you,
And pull you closer,
But I think you're too scared I'll drift away with the tide,
And you'll never see me again.

I'll be here 'till the end, my darling,
I can promise you that much.
At least I think I can.
I'm not quite as sure these days.

You know, I've been writing you a poem.
The first lines are a bit blurry behind the ocean mist,
And I've mostly forgotten what it was supposed mean,
But it's from me and made just for your eyes alone,
And I think that's all that truly matters.

I don't know if I've told you yet, but I love you.
I can't quite remember who you are,
But I perfectly recall that I've always loved
Every little thing about you.
And how could I not?

HEIDI THOMPSON

Because standing here, on the edge of oblivion,
The cruel wind drying up the tears I can't even remember
shedding,
The salty air cleansing my lungs
Of the fear that has polluted them for centuries,
And with your trembling but grounding fingers
Entwining with my own weakening touch,
I couldn't feel more at peace.

Shoreham by Sea, July 13, 2023

LONESOME TRAVELLER

Tortured wind shrieked beyond the walls,
Rattling the windowpanes with every sharp beating from the rain.
The heavy blackness of the night left no room for light,
Masking him as he ascended the step.

When the first knock came, I thought it was merely the wind.
The night's monsters will never let up on his poor soul.
Once I did go to check though,
A man stood, framed in the coldness of the night.

Just passing through.
His voice was raspy and odd, yet soft in a way
One can only be after centuries
Of cold bones and even colder hearts.

I sat him down on my old oak chair,
Draped a battered blanket around his hunched and beaten back.
It stood like the mountains on which the morning suns rise,
After decades burdened by the bags he carries with him.

Heavier still, I saw the weight upon those eyes.
On some day, they must have shone like stars
To illuminate this cold and weary night,
But the branches coiling around his feet
Tore him from the sky.

Have something to eat.

Those once bright eyes flickered around the room,
Memorising every escape and hiding place
In case the dinner went sour.

His actions were rehearsed as he ate.
Perhaps, just months before,
Those orders had been barked at him
By an army general:

Hurry up, you ain't got forever!
The enemy doesn't wait to attack!
He thanked me profusely as I led him into a spare room
And I thought,
When was the last time he'd slept in peace?

By the time he left upon dawn next morning,
The rain had let up for a bit,
And I watched him limp back into the impassive night.
I pondered to myself for many days after that,
What heavy past could weigh on such a burdened soul?

Shoreham by Sea, July 14, 2023

EPHEMERAL

We were always meant to be short-lived.
I knew it from the moment we met.
Forest green eyes travelled downward,
And shy cerulean ones floated upwards with a hesitant glint,
To meet at the middle.
I thought then, this.
This small little space in between,
This is where I want to spend my days.
I know with a strange kind of conviction,
That from the moment you first opened your eyes,
So incomplete, as were my own,
Without each other's sight burned into their very core,
Everybody knew that you would be a rebel.
And how wouldn't you be?
As fate spun the silver threads of your life,
Weaving in long, drawn-out times of war
And fleeting flashes of devastation and grief
That left your mind reeling and spinning off its axis,
It was all that's kept you fighting for this long,
Long enough for me to be lying here,
Awake, though it's the middle of the night,
Staring idly at your dark silhouette asleep beside me.
As the filtered moonlight kissed your face,
Highlighting your every last perfect imperfection,
And framing you in a glowing halo of the creeping dusk,
I realized once again that this,
This is how I want to go.
Today, though, we stand here,

After so many days surrounded by the Sun
And the keening silver moon,
And we've finally learned to appreciate the stars.
Not even so long ago
I begged like a prayer
For you to stay, here, with me,
But now, at this moment, I'm finally at peace.
I breathe in one last breath,
A final kiss drawn from your sweetly familiar lips.
My roaming fingertips find and connect with your own,
Drinking in your shining blue eyes one last time
As we tread off into the night.
Our ashes and bones scatter across the sky.
It's as you've always wished, my love:
Our souls are here, eternally together,
And the ghost of our touch lingers
On the weeping magnolia bushes.
We whisper to each other as the wind
That brushes over our bones,
And the bones of others
Sighing woefully beside us.

Budapest, July 17, 2023

HIRAETH

I think I'll finally let you go.
I've spent every waking hour of the past few years
Trying desperately, with every strand of my will,
To keep holding onto you.
I deserve to finally realize
There hasn't really been anything to hold onto.
Nevertheless, I clutch carefully at your boneless fingers,
Lain listlessly on the off-white hospital sheets,
As if scared, by squeezing too hard,
I'll be the one to bring about your death.
Our hearts beat in tandem with the wind
As it rustles past the quivering willow tree outside your window,
Almost as if reminding it it won't be there forever.
My throat is closing up painfully again,
And for a brief moment, I think that maybe
I'm the one who's dying.
You have made me so much wiser, in every way of the word,
Than anyone I expected it from ever has.
I still rely on you to teach me
How I'm supposed to let you go.
You told me yesterday, somewhere around noon,
That we were all just visitors on Earth,
And that afterward, we would be here to water it
For the next lucky few who passed by.
And I know this... this body of yours
Was still so heart-achingly young,
But as I sit here, beside its frayed and distorted shell,
I know with all the conviction there is

That you are not still in there.
It also makes me wonder,
Just how old is your soul?
I know you were only twenty-six,
Yet I'd consider you an old person.
And I don't imagine a shrinking form and battered eyes,
And baggy flesh refusing to retreat
Back onto your rattling bones.
I imagine the thousands of years you have spent on Earth
Before me.
Because when it comes down to it,
Is it really just the age,
Countable in the heavy lines that living
Carves into your very pores?
Or is it something more than that.
I'm afraid this is the end, but I know
That somehow, some way,
We will find each other again,
And again,
And again.
And I need you to teach me to let go,
Even if, in this life,
I do not yet know how.

Budapest, July 20, 2023

STAY

This is the end. I just know it.
It was all going to come together eventually.
I'm crying and sobbing and begging,
Please. Please, don't go.
I'm telling the universe,
I need somewhere to stay.
Somewhere I know is my home.
The pale grey of the sky shifts in protest above me,
Unravelling, like yarn, before my feet.
And the soil turns, and churns,
And crumbles between my toes,
And thorny rose bushes climb their way up my spine.
The Sun burns brighter, and brighter, and brighter.
Eventually, I have to force myself to look away,
Before I am turned to ash with everything else
In existence.
But the sky is fine.
It sparkles an easy cerulean blue
As a horde of seagulls draw a line across its chest.
The earth is intact,
And the Sun is completely okay.
I look down at my fingertips, unmarred, but trembling softly.
And in the distance by now,
You are walking away.

Budapest, July 21, 2023

QUIET LOVE

I never feel like I'm wasting time with you.
Sitting here, in this small corner of the world
Silence, like a blanket, sits upon us,
As the autumn leaves upon the frost-bitten soil.
We will say nothing, yet it'll still feel
So full,
So special,
So alive.
You are gentle love.
You'll watch the sunlight caress my face
Over our morning coffee,
Just to trace it afterwards
With the warmth of your own touch.
You are slow love
That finds me in the dark,
And searches the empty space between us
To hold my hand on sweat-soaked summer nights,
To say goodnight
Without disturbing the hush.
I am the answer
That will grab onto it wordlessly,
And pass it back to you.
I am the word
That wants to love you loudly,
In front of everyone,
And then quiet again,
Just between us.
  -Budapest, July 24, 2023

HEAR ME

I am the whisper,
Hiding beneath the cruel winds
As they shriek past the house.
I am the plea
That stares helplessly through the window
On this night of rueful terror.
I am the cry
That asks why it cannot be seen,
But does not hear the cacophony
Sounding all around it.
You are the word
As the rain begins to falter,
And the wind trips suddenly over its steps.
You are the reply
To my bleeding, unhearing ears.
Why can they not hear me?
I can.
Yours is the only voice I hear beyond the haze, and
You are the reply.

Budapest, July 24, 2023

SUDDENLY

For months, perhaps even a year at this point,
I have been drifting.
My feet do not touch the ground,
But something invisible blocks me
From reaching for the stars.
I'm not quite certain what has caused it,
And I wasn't sure I'd ever return home.
It was an abrupt and unexpected change,
Leaving my mind reeling, and suddenly
I was crashing to the ground,
Right into your outstretched arms.
Where did you come from?
I may never know.
All I know is that suddenly,
It was no longer off-toned dinners spent alone,
Eating in silence, feeling something was off,
But not realizing how lonely it was
Before it suddenly wasn't.
Suddenly, in a flash like the last bolt of lightning
At the end of a night-long storm,
It was no longer chilly mornings,
Hunched over a half-cold cup of coffee,
Humming an annoyingly slow song to fill the silence,
And restless nights in a large, oddly empty bed,
Eating me up whole.
I am your creation, and perhaps you were the missing piece
To the porcelain heart you've created for me.
I am your creation, and so I cannot lie to you,

And say I don't know,
You will be my destruction.

Budapest, July 24, 2023

THE ORCHARD OF
SILENT DEVOTION

Our love was never loud.
It bloomed in the quiet,
Dark corners of the greenhouse,
But it was real.

Warm touches in the cold, unrelenting nights,
Flowers blossoming where our fingertips met,
As if we were attempting to create an orchard
Of our teenage passions.

We didn't grow up.
We grew together like two roses,
Entwining, interlocking, dancing
In the eternal dance of sweet sunshine
And warm soil beneath us.

We didn't cry when it rained,
But we laughed.
Laughed at how odd it was
That anyone could feel beaten down
By the way it pours down on you
And washes you away,
Leaving not a hair,
Not a single pore of you unclean.

We get it now,
But somehow, those bad days,
Those loud, brash furies
Stretching out into eternity
And stealing the short, quiet seconds
We saved to treasure for ourselves,

And the cold wind's hazy ghosts
Of unrelenting sadness
Soaking through to our bones,
Making us shiver through the endless night,
They only seemed to fuel the Sun to burn brighter,
To make up for lost minutes
And wasted hours.

Our love was never seen,
But it bloomed, invisible,
Invincible as the day.

Budapest, July 24, 2023

REMINDERS

Every day, people say,
"You could lose this kind of love."
And every day I laugh,
And I smile politely, and I think,
I could never lose what we have.
Because you could be separated by oceans,
Miles of mountains and galaxies of stars,
Or simply just the unstoppable march of time,
And yet I'd still see you in everything,
Everywhere I went.
I'd see you in the knots of clouds,
Floating away from each other,
Giving way for the Sun to shine down on me,
With the warmth of your body against mine.
I'd see you in freshly mowed lawns,
And the chirping of the morning birds
As they happily await your return.
I'd be reminded of you over and over,
Every single time I saw a group of kids
Laughing innocently on the neighbourhood streets
Under the cheerful sun,
Because you always brought out that same
Childish side in me
That I never got to see before.
And I would never really mind these reminders,
Because it would mean I could laugh
In the face of fate
For ever thinking it could keep us apart.
  -Budapest, July 28, 2023

FIREFLIES

I don't usually appreciate the silences
Between sentences,
And when our words lull and drop heavily in the dirt
When we have nothing left to say.
But tonight is different.
Tonight is not a lack.
There is nothing missing
From the way we sit beside each other
In the warmth of the evening breeze.
Tonight is about filling in the blanks
Of everything we don't say
In the confusion and rush of the day.
Not with words, just movements of the night.
Palm trees all around us whisper gently
Of our love.
They know the tales of how we got here,
So they know to keep their voices to a hush,
Barely grazed by the wind.
The past has told us wisely
To not take it too fast,
So instead, your fingers find mine,
And my hand roams to wrap
Carefully around your shoulder,
Using soft touches as our kisses,
Without ever opening our mouths.
My bare feet slosh anxiously, slowly,
In the cool black water of the pond,
Occasionally bumping into yours.
We both look up, you bite down on your smile.

I'm confused on why you would,
But I grin back, nonetheless.
You are beautiful like this.
Illuminated only by the faint light
Of the fireflies and the milky moon,
Sighing somewhere above us.
It's not quite akin to when the filtered morning Sun
Shifts into a golden halo around your head,
Framing your entire being in its light,
But there may be something in not knowing
Anything other than your face.
The cicadas hum peacefully,
In beat with our breathing,
A slow intake as we exhale out
All our tense muscles and
Nervously tapping fingertips.
I watch in a trance as your eyes follow
The trail a little duck draws on the pond's inky surface.
You pick it up as gently as the breeze,
Tiny, soft feathers and a small little beak
Nesting among your fingertips.
Seeing the creature, so at home between your arms,
I cannot help falling in love
All over again.
When the kiss finally comes,
Your lips are a little hesitant.
Like a touch, pressing down on a fresh wound,
I feel that I am finally healing,
Down to my weakest bones.

Budapest, July 29, 2023

HAIKUS

December 21, 2022

The clock is ticking.
My mask is slipping further,
I feel like running.

Just keep on writing.
My thoughts are slipping away,
Memories are gone.

May 7, 2023

Told me you'd return
as you faded away.
When will you be back?

Could you hold my hand?
I need you here with me now,
while I say goodbye.

I'll scream, sob and shout,
but I'll never know how to
wake up without you.

Devils don't cry, we
scream 'till our throats are raw, and
God lends us mercy.

One last breath in was
all I ever needed to
get away from you.

Seven nations fell,
and seven worlds burned to the ground
in the name of peace.

You are the reason
for which I fell, but you are
also why now, I fly.

To bury a friend
is the loneliest of fates,
and I am sorry.

Let's rewrite the stars,
and prove our fates as options,
never to come true.

A dead man's song is
a symphony of notes that

you will never hear.

I'll always stand here,
await you for a lifetime,
weep when you don't show.

Three ways this could end,
two that you would never choose,
one that dooms us all.

Your voice is fragile,
and moments from breaking,
but louder than you think.

Blue sky above me,
deep, dark pits below me, but
just one road to walk.

When the Devil's scared,
run. You do not want to know
who you're running from.

May 8, 2023

No one saw his face,
his name was never said aloud,
but everyone knew.

I can't remember
What I lost, but its fear is
Keeping me alive.

June 13, 2023

Dance with me, my love.
Pull at my strings, and pull at
the strings of my heart.

Lay with me, my love.
A field of poppies poking
through our yellowed bones.

Watch me drown, my love.
Throw me in the ocean, and
watch me take a breath.

See me fall, my love.
I stood, and I flew, and I
Fell for only you.

Brother, let me go.
Once you leave, I'll guide you and
Show you where to go.

Beware of young gods.
They still think they can die, so
They fight for their lives.

Let me hold you on
Broken nights like these, and I'll
Sing you back to sleep.

I know you still watch
Over me. Please look away; I
Don't want you to see.

I don't like waiting
In line, but I'll wait for
Your heart any time.

August 2, 2023

In your shattered-winged
Embrace, you rule my heart, and
I swear you rule the world.

Men will pray to God,
But there is one angel who
Still just prays to man.

The night saw his gaze
Was dark, cradling freezing hands,
And a frozen heart.

You've loved watching the
butterflies dance long before he
chained you to the ground.

Glancing at him now,
he fades off before your eyes,
just another ghost.

I think I'm a ghost.
It's why, with every glance, I
fade more from your mind.

We aren't soulmates. Stars
don't align when we touch, but
we're an act of spite.

Two huge, yellow eyes
piercing through my heart and flesh,
staring down my soul.

The cat stands still. Black
tail curling 'round the moon, it
rips it from the sky.

"Never again," she
said, over and over. She's

still stuck in that loop.

My heart has caved in.
My mind is breaking, yet still,
you don't seem to mind.

The moth in the night
constantly, incessantly
scavenging for light.

Standing on a rock,
ankles swallowed by the waves, I
shiver to my bones.

Tear's touch on my cheek.
It trickles down my chin, and
freezes on my skin.

Highways embrace him,
drifting onwards every night
under bruising skies.

Don't blame God when he
cries. Just look what we've done to
his best creation.

A grave truth pours from
your lips at last, as the empty
swallows you up.

Why'd it take so long
for you to tell me? We could
have been forever.

She almost told him.
He almost got there in time,
and they almost lived.

Why do you still cry?

HEIDI THOMPSON

I know this is goodbye, but I can
finally tell my truth.

It's been a long time.
You still haven't returned, so
maybe I should leave.

Shiver in the snow.
I wrap my arms around you.
Pause to take a breath.

Silent is the night,
silent are the moon's tears as
dusk swallows your bones.

The moon takes not a
breath, nor do the stars dare blink
while you lie, asleep.

What could I say, what
could ever convince you that
I am still right here?

It's just three simple
words, yet here I am, choking
on my every breath.

Printed in Great Britain
by Amazon

30190058R00046